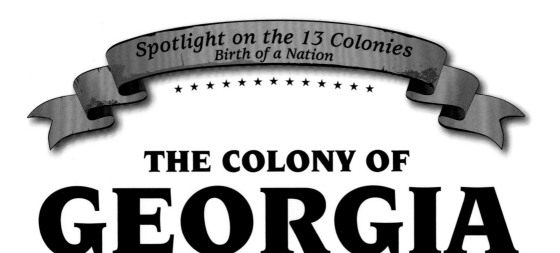

Spotlight on the 13 Colonies
Birth of a Nation

★ ★ ★ ★ ★ ★ ★ ★ ★ ★ ★ ★

THE COLONY OF
GEORGIA

Sarah Machajewski

PowerKiDS
press™

NEW YORK

Published in 2016 by The Rosen Publishing Group, Inc.
29 East 21st Street, New York, NY 10010

Editor: Sarah Machajewski
Book Design: Andrea Davison-Bartolotta

Photo Credits: Cover, pp. 16–17, 19 North Wind Picture Archives; p. 4 John Sartain/Wikimedia Commons; p. 5 I. Pilon/Shutterstock.com; p. 7 The Print Collector/Hulton Archive/Getty Images; p. 8 Thomas Hudson/National Portrait Gallery/Wikimedia Commons; p. 9 courtesy of Georgia Archives; p. 10 Interim Archives/Archive Photos/Getty Images; p. 11 courtesy of the Library of Congress; p. 13 Buyenlarge/Archive Photos/Getty Images; pp. 14–15 (both) Bubba 73/Wikimedia Commons; p. 18 British Library/Wikimedia Commons; pp. 20–21 Hulton Archive/Getty Images; p. 22 VectorPic/Shutterstock.com.

Library of Congress Cataloging-in-Publication Data

Machajewski, Sarah.
The colony of Georgia / by Sarah Machajewski.
p. cm. — (Spotlight on the 13 colonies: Birth of a nation)
Includes index.
ISBN 978-1-4994-0493-7 (pbk.)
ISBN 978-1-4994-0497-5 (6 pack)
ISBN 978-1-4994-0494-4 (library binding)
1. Georgia — History — Colonial period, ca. 1600-1775 — Juvenile literature. 2. Georgia — History — 1775-1865 — Juvenile literature. 3. Georgia — History — Colonial period, ca. 1600-1775. I. Machajewski, Sarah. II. Title.
F289.M33 2016
975.8'02—d23

Manufactured in the United States of America

CPSIA Compliance Information: Batch #WS15PK: For further information contact Rosen Publishing, New York, New York at 1-800-237-9932.

Contents

Claiming Land in the New World

In October 1492, Christopher Columbus reached islands he thought were in Asia. They were actually part of the Americas, which Europeans called the New World. Soon, leaders of European countries sent explorers to the New World in search of riches and land to claim as their own. This land included the area that would later become the colony of Georgia.

One of the first Europeans known to have come to Georgia was Spanish explorer Hernando de Soto in 1540. He came in search of gold, but didn't find it. He did, however, claim land for Spain. Spain didn't colonize Georgia at this time, but didn't want other Europeans coming onto their territory. The Spanish

Hernando de Soto

built military outposts, called forts, along the coast to protect their land. These forts, such as the one built in 1566 on St. Catherines Island on the coast of Georgia, allowed Spain to control the southeast Atlantic coast for almost 200 years. Then, in 1733, Britain established its thirteenth and last colony in America—Georgia.

This map shows where the Georgia colony was located.

A Land of Second Chances

By the early 1700s, Britain had already established 12 colonies in North America. South Carolina was the southernmost colony and was **vulnerable** to attacks from the Spanish in Florida, the French in Louisiana, and native tribes in the area. The British government felt South Carolina needed something to protect it.

Meanwhile, a member of the British **Parliament**, James Oglethorpe, was spending his time helping the poor and people who were in **debt**. Debtors went to jail when they couldn't pay back what they owed. In 1732, Oglethorpe came up with an idea for how to help them instead of sending them to jail. He thought Britain should establish a new colony in the territory between South Carolina and Florida. The new colony would act as protection against attacks, but it could also be a place where the poor and debtors could have a second chance at life. The colony would be named Georgia, after Britain's King George II.

James Oglethorpe

James Oglethorpe was the man behind the creation of Georgia, Britain's thirteenth and last colony.

Establishing the Colony

Oglethorpe and 20 men, known as the Georgia Trustees, asked King George II to grant them land to establish a colony for the poor and debtors. The king agreed to the idea. The Trustees received a **charter** from the king and funding from Parliament in June 1732.

The king's charter gave the Trustees the powers of a corporation, which meant they could elect a governing body for the colony, grant land, and establish their own laws and taxes. The charter was good for 21 years. After that, Georgia would become a royal colony run by the king.

The Trustees came up with a plan to give 50 acres (20 ha) of land to people in need, under the condition that they would settle the land themselves and help build the colony. These people couldn't sell their land or borrow money against it. People could also buy land in Georgia, but since it was supposed to be a place to benefit the poor, they couldn't purchase more than 500 acres (203 ha).

King George II

George the Second by the Grace of God of Great Britain France & Ireland King Defender of the Faith & To all to whom these Presents shall come Greeting Whereas We are Credibly informed Many of Our Poor Subjects are through Misfortunes and Want of Employment reduced to great Necessities insomuch as by their Labour they are not Able to Provide a Maintenance for themselves and Familys and if they had Means to defray the Charge of Passage and other Expences incident to New Settlements they would be Glad to be Settled in any of Our Provinces in America where by Cultivating the Lands at Present Wast and Desolate they Might not only Gain a comfortable Subsistance for themselves and Familys but also Strengthen Our Colonys and Encreas the Trade Navigation and Wealth of these Our Realms And Whereas Our Provinces in North America have been frequently Ravaged by Indian Enemies More Especially that of South Carolina which in the last Warr by the Neighbouring Savages was laid Wast with fire and Sword and Great Numbers of the English Inhabitants Miserable Massacred and Our loving Subjects who now Inhabit them by reason of the Smallness of ther Numbe[r] of any new Warr be Exposed to the like Ca[lamities] much as their whole Southern Frontier [continueth] Unsettled and lyeth Open to the Said Sa[vages] Whereas We think it highly becoming [Our] Royal Dignity to Protect all Our Lovi[ng Subjects be] they Never so Distant from Us to extend O[ur] Fatherly Compassion Even to the Meanest & Most Unfortuna[te] of Our People and to relieve the Wants of Our Abovemen tioned Poor Subjects and that it will be highly

9

This image shows a page of the charter for Georgia granted to the Trustees by George II.

The Savannah Settlement

The Georgia Trustees planned Georgia as a debtors' colony, but they wanted to choose who settled there. They wanted colonists whose skills could help build the colony, such as farmers, carpenters, bakers, and more. By the time all the colonists were selected, there wasn't one debtor among them.

Oglethorpe and 114 settlers set sail for Georgia in November 1732. They arrived in February 1733 and chose to settle on Yamacraw Bluff—a steep hill overlooking the Savannah River. A group of Yamacraw Indians was already living there. Oglethorpe became friendly with their chief, Tomochichi, who allowed the colonists to settle on Yamacraw Bluff. They named their settlement Savannah.

With the help of the **militia** and slaves from South Carolina, the land was cleared of trees. Oglethorpe drew up a plan for Savannah. He separated the land into squares and planned for **identical** houses on them. Some squares were used for public buildings. The identical lots and houses were meant to prevent rich and poor classes from forming.

Oglethorpe meets with Tomochichi

With everything meant to be equal and evenly given out to settlers, Savannah was planned to be a place of social equality.

Rules in Georgia Colony

Life in the new colony of Georgia wasn't easy. The early settlers faced a host of troubles. Many colonists died within the first year, and the crops they planted didn't produce as much as they had expected.

One of the biggest struggles colonists faced was living under the rules, laws, and **restrictions** the Trustees had established for the colony. The Georgia Trustees had a very clear idea of what they wanted Georgia to be and created laws to make sure it happened. These included restrictions on the amount of land colonists could own, rules about **inheritance** that kept colonists from growing the size of their estates, and laws against bringing in or manufacturing rum.

Also, unlike the other colonies, there was no system of self-government in Georgia, so the colonists had no say in how the colony was run. Finally, the Georgia Trustees banned slavery. This was to prevent large **plantations** from forming along with large gaps between the rich and the poor. These laws led to bad feelings between the colonists and the Trustees.

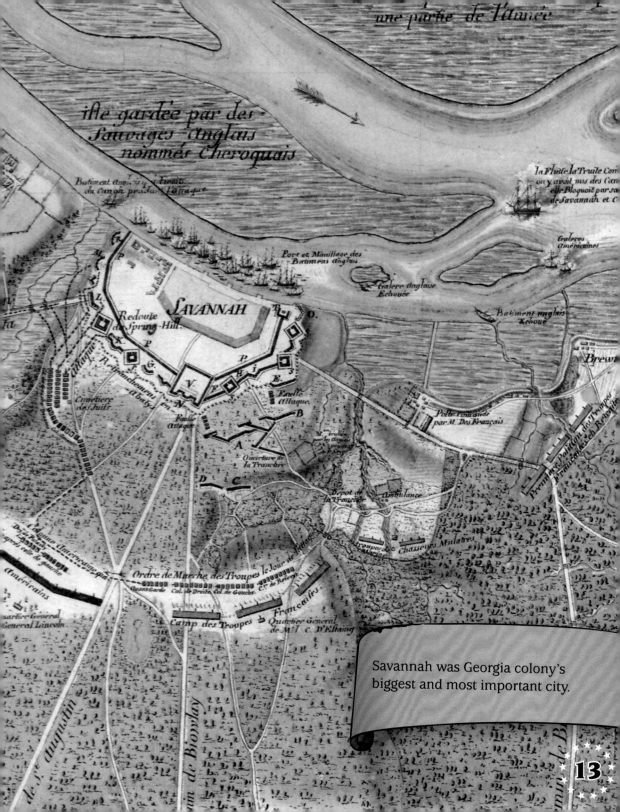

une partie de l'armée

isle gardée par des
sauvages anglais
nommés Cheroquais

la Fluite la Truite Con
on y avoit mis des Cen
elle Bloquoit par so
de Savannah et C

Batiment Anglais y a Truite
du Canon pres de l'Ataque

Galeres
Américaines

Port et Mouillage des
Batimens anglais

SAVANNAH

Galere anglaise
Echouée

Batiment anglais
Echoué

Redoute
du Spring-Hill.

Ataque
Retranchement D'ataque

Cimetiere
des Juifs

Fausse
Attaque

Faute
Attaque

Brew

Ouverture de
la Tranchée

Batiment des
Ambulance

Poste Occupée
par M. Des Français

Dépôt de
la Tranchée

Premiere Position des Troupes
Françaises en Redoute

Colonne Américaine

Troupes des Chasseurs Mulatres

Colonne Américaine
à gauche

Ordre de Marche des Troupes le Jour de l'attaque

Avantgarde   Col. de Droite Col. de Gauche   C. de Réserve

Américains

Quartier Général
Général Lincoln

Camp des Troupes
Françaises

Quartier Général
de M. le C. D'Estaing

chem de Brewlay

Savannah was Georgia colony's
biggest and most important city.

Fighting to Survive

As Britain's southernmost colony, Georgia was in a location that left it vulnerable to attacks by the Spanish. The Spanish and the British fought each other over territory in Georgia. They also fought over control of the seas. One encounter was particularly bloody. In 1731, a Spanish patrol boat captured a British ship. The Spanish commander accused the British captain, Robert Jenkins, of **smuggling** and cut off his ear! This led to a war between Britain and Spain in 1739—the War of Jenkins' Ear.

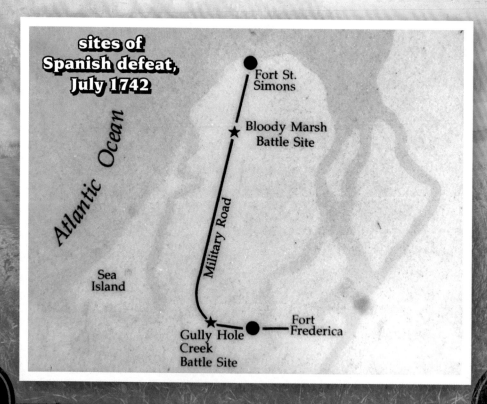

sites of Spanish defeat, July 1742

Atlantic Ocean

Fort St. Simons

Bloody Marsh Battle Site

Military Road

Sea Island

Gully Hole Creek Battle Site

Fort Frederica

James Oglethorpe led British efforts against the Spanish. He launched attacks and guided troops in battle. He also took control of two Spanish forts in Florida. The Battle of Bloody Marsh in 1742 secured a British victory, and the war ended in 1743. A few attacks happened after that, but the two countries agreed to stop fighting in 1748. These efforts were extremely important to the success of Georgia colony. Had the British not won, the colony would probably have failed or fallen under Spanish rule.

This image shows how the site of the Battle of Bloody Marsh looks today.

Becoming Royal

Over time, colonists became increasingly unhappy with life in Georgia. Many felt the limit on land ownership prevented them from becoming rich. The ban on slavery was one of the most disliked laws. Settlers who had come from colonies that had slavery, such as South Carolina, knew how much money they could earn with a plantation and slave labor. They wanted those opportunities in Georgia, too.

The Trustees slowly relaxed their policies on land ownership, inheritance, and rum. In 1750, they lifted the ban on slavery. This encouraged more people to settle in Georgia. Soon, plantations and slave labor became major parts of the colony's economy. Rice and cotton became the most important crops. Also, the Trustees invited colonists to choose **delegates** for a **representative** assembly that would advise the Trustees on what the colonists wanted. However, they couldn't make laws themselves.

Despite these changes, colonists were still unhappy with the Trustees. The Trustees decided to give up ownership of Georgia one year before the charter **expired**. In 1752, Georgia was turned over to King George II, and it became a royal colony.

Once it became a royal colony, Georgia was ruled by a governor and council that were nominated by a committee of Parliament and approved by the king. The colony also had an elected assembly whose members were chosen by the colonists.

The Issue of Taxes

As a royal colony, Georgia was subjected to the same rules and regulations as the other 12 British colonies. That included taxation. From 1754 to 1763, Britain and France fought over land in North America in the French and Indian War. Britain won, but the war was expensive. Britain decided to tax the colonists to help pay for the war. The money would also pay for keeping British soldiers in the colonies to maintain peace between colonists and Native Americans.

Britain imposed a tax on many kinds of goods, including tea and sugar. One of the most notable taxes was the Stamp Act of 1765. It required colonists to pay a tax on every piece of paper they used. Colonists hadn't been allowed to vote on the tax, which made many of them angry. Some colonists, including Georgians, joined the Sons of Liberty, a group that protested the Stamp Act and other taxes. Representatives from nine colonies gathered and adopted 14 **resolutions** about their rights. Georgia wasn't among them. Governor James Wright tried to block any efforts by Georgians to oppose the Stamp Act.

one-penny tax stamp used on newspapers

Colonists take to the streets to protest the Stamp Act. It was so unpopular that Britain did away with it in 1766.

The Colonies Unite

Over the next 10 years, the idea of becoming an independent nation started to spread. Colonists who wanted independence were called patriots. Colonists who remained loyal to Britain were called loyalists. Many Georgians were loyalists. It was the youngest colony, and its ties to Britain were still strong.

In 1774, representatives from 12 colonies gathered in Philadelphia to discuss their issues with Britain. This became known as the First Continental Congress. Georgia was the only colony that didn't **participate**. Then, in April 1775, fighting broke out between British soldiers and American patriots at Lexington and Concord in Massachusetts. This event, known as the Battles of Lexington and Concord, began the American Revolution.

The Second Continental Congress met in May 1775 to discuss what steps to take next. Georgia didn't participate at first, though a man named Lyman Hall attended as an unofficial delegate. In July, Georgians voted on whether or not to join the cause. They voted yes, and official delegates from Georgia colony arrived at the Second Continental Congress on July 20. The American colonies declared their independence a year later, on July 4, 1776.

This image shows members of the Second Continental Congress meeting to discuss American independence.

The United States of America

The American Revolution lasted from 1775 to 1783. Few Georgians joined the army because most of the battles took place in other colonies. Additionally, many Georgians were still loyalists.

The first battle in Georgia was in 1776. British troops attacked American ships in Savannah's harbor and stole the rice that was on board. In 1778, the British took over Savannah entirely. They remained there until 1782. However, fighting had ended in 1781 when the Continental army beat the British in Yorktown, Virginia.

The American Revolution ended when Britain and the new United States signed the Treaty of Paris in 1783. In 1787, leaders from each state met to discuss the United States' set of laws, which was called the Articles of Confederation. William Few, Abraham Baldwin, William Houstoun, and William Leigh Pierce represented Georgia. The meeting resulted in writing a new set of laws, called the Constitution, which is still used by the United States today. On January 2, 1788, Georgia accepted the new Constitution and became the fourth state to join the new nation.

Glossary

charter: A piece of writing from a king or other leader that grants or guarantees something.

debt: Something owed by one person to another, such as money.

delegate: A person sent to a meeting or convention to represent others.

expire: To come to an end.

identical: Exactly the same.

inheritance: Something that's received after the death of the previous owner.

militia: A group of citizen soldiers who are trained and ready to fight when needed.

Parliament: The name of the United Kingdom's legislative branch, which includes the House of Commons and House of Lords.

participate: To take part in.

plantation: Large farms on which cotton, tobacco, or sugarcane are grown.

representative: Someone who is chosen to act or speak for other people.

resolution: A formal expression of an opinion.

restriction: A limitation.

smuggling: Sneaking something into or out of a place illegally.

vulnerable: At risk.

Index

Primary Source List

Page 8. *King George II.* Created by Thomas Hudson. Oil on canvas. 1744. Now kept at the National Portrait Gallery, London, United Kingdom.

Page 9. *The Royal Charter Incorporating the Trustees for Establishing the Colony of Georgia in America.* Recorded by the Secretary of the Province of South Carolina from a copy carried to Georgia by James Oglethorpe. February 22, 1735. Now kept at the Georgia Archives and Records Building, Murrow, GA.

Page 11. *A view of Savanah as it stood the 29th of March, 1734.* Created by Pierre Fourdrinier. Engraving based on a drawing by Peter Gordon. 1735. Now kept at the Library of Congress Prints and Photographs Division, Washington, D.C.

Page 13. *Siège de Savannah fait par les troupes françoises aux ordres du général d'Estaing vice-amiral de France, en 7.bre, et 8.bre 1779.* Created by Pierre Ozanne. Pen and ink and watercolor on paper. 1779. Now kept at the Library of Congress Geography and Maps Division, Washington, D.C.

Page 18. One-penny stamp for newspaper paper to be sold by government agents in colonies. Created by the Board of Stamps. Proof impression from sheet of proofs. Ink on paper. 1765. Now kept at the British Library Philatelic Collections, London, United Kingdom.

Pages 20–21. *Congress Voting the Declaration of Independence.* Created around 1817 by Edward Savage. Engraving based on a painting by Robert Edge Pine, ca. 1776.

Websites